Co

Title Page ....
Special Thanks ....
Copyright 3
Contents 4
CHAPTER ONE Intro 5
CHAPTER TWO Using your controller 7
CHAPTER THREE Deciding on a mixer/controller 10
CHAPTER FOUR Controller Techniques 13
CHAPTER FIVE Creating your first real mix 15
CHAPTER SIX Finding Your Streaming Site 17
CHAPTER SEVEN Your Stage Name 19
CHAPTER EIGHT Finding your First Gig 21
CHAPTER NINE Marketing and Branding 23
CHAPTER TEN Outro 25
CHAPTER ELEVEN The Secret Chapter 27
About the Author 28

Become a DJ in 60 days:

And Get Paid Doing It!

by D.D. Graston

1

Special Thanks

I want to thank my parents Sherrie and Tom for all that they have done for me in life, and all of the support they have given over the years.

I also want to thank my girlfriend Ashley, who loves, inspires, and encourages me every day to do better in my work and in my life.

Without these people this publication wouldn't have been possible. Thank you.

Copyright © 2018 by D.D. Graston
All rights reserved. This book or any portion thereof
may not be reproduced or used in any manner whatsoever
without the express written permission of the publisher
except for the use of brief quotations in a book review.
Printed in the United States of America

ISBN: 9781983200229
Graston Publishing
446 Laurel Street,
Reno, NV 89512

Contents

Intro: What this book can do for you

Chapter 2: Finding a mixer / controller that's right for you and your budget

Chapter 3: Learning to use your controller

Chapter 4: Controller techniques

Chapter 5: Creating your first mixes

Chapter 6: Finding the best streaming site that suits your style

Chapter 7: Coming up with your brand name

Chapter 8: Finding your first gigs

Chapter 9: Marketing and branding

Outro: Final thoughts, and further reading

CHAPTER ONE
Intro

<u>What This Book Can Do For You</u>

Let me start by explaining who this text is for: this book is for anyone new looking to get started into DJing, budding DJs looking for new tips, and veterans looking to gain a new insight on the industry. Basically, this book will have something to gain for anyone and everyone reading it. I make this important distinction because we in the music industry get caught up focusing on our own techniques without continuously learning the newest tips and tricks. There are so many fantastic options, both paid and free to continue on. Without YouTube, podcasts, blogs, and many EDM forums I would not be where I am today both skill and career-wise. Which leads me to my next discussion…

This book can do a lot for getting you on the right track, but nothing will happen without the participation and hard work needed by you to get there. The one thing I tell everyone starting out in this business is to be persistent, no matter what point you are at in life you can achieve your goals if you persist and set your sights on it. Don't let anyone or anything stand in your way, you've only got one life, take control of it.

Now with my ranting out of the way we can get down to it: this book will cover everything from finding a mixer/ controller that's right for you and your budget, learning to use your mixer, controller techniques, creating your first mixes, finding the best streaming site that suits your style, coming up with your brand name, finding your first gigs, and marketing and branding tips to get you recognized.

If you can follow this simple book for 60 days I guarantee you will be on your way to becoming a master. staying on course with the daily 2-3 hours can be hard, but squeeze it in after work, after school, or early in the morning. Whatever you do, practice! This book contains all of the steps needed to get far as a professional DJ, but if you can't put the time in to sit down and learn everyday these tools and tips won't do anything for you. Practice makes a professional. If you miss any days, try and add that time you missed to the next day's practice. Contained in the back of this book is a cheat sheet for helping you stay on track with what you should be practicing or doing week by week.

CHAPTER TWO
Using your controller

Learning to use your controller

Almost every controller is different and I'm not going to be able to get to every feature, that comes down to you. You have to put in the time to learn your specific controller. Read the manual, watch a few videos on it, but most importantly spend time playing around on it. The more familiar and comfortable you get with your device, the better you will become! With that being said, let's get down to basics. Almost every DJ controller has a jog wheel; many have two jog wheels. They typically look like a vinyl record or a large circular disk. This is primarily used to scratch or for temporarily adjusting tempo. Next, your controller will have a slider either to the side of the jog wheel or beneath it. This slider is used to slow down/speed up the tempo of a song making it either go slower or faster.

Your controller might have a set of rubber pads with the words: CUE, LOOP, and SAMPLER. First, Cue is used to return to points in a song that you have set up or cued. You can use this to jump around to a specific moment in the songs you are using. Next, we have Loop which may contain auto loop and manual loop depending on your controller. The loop function is used to loop a spot in a song allowing you to mix in another song or build your own drop. The auto loop function uses predetermined beats to loop, while the manual loop allows you to customize your own to any shape or length. Lastly, we have the Sampler. The sampler is some DJs favorite tool, but don't fall into the trap of over using samples and sounding like a cheesy radio broadcaster. The sampler allows you to play previously loaded sounds and clips by pressing the appropriate pads associated with each sample.

Your controller will most likely have a "Sync" button, which when pressed, changes the BPM (Beats Per Minute) of the newly loaded song to match the BPM of the currently playing song. The play/pause button should be straightforward, as it both plays and pauses the song depending on if the file is already playing or not. Next you will have your plug inputs either behind, or on the side of the deck. These inputs could include an XLR cable which is circular with three prongs inside, an RCA cable which is the white and red plugs, or it could be a 1/4" Auxiliary (AUX) plug. Your controller will also have a headphone input to allow you to cue up your next song in the mix without anyone else hearing it.

In the middle of your controller should be some knobs, you should have three knobs marked with the words "Hi" "Mid" and "Low". This is your equalizer (EQ, EQ Knobs) which allows you to decrease or increase your outputs at the different frequencies. For instance, turning up your Low will increase your Bass output (Always watch your levels either on the software or your hardware if you are pushing your equalizer to the max, you don't want to blow your speakers!). Below the EQ knobs your controller might have a knob for Low Pass Filter (lpf) and High Pass Filter (hpf). The Low Pass Filter allows low frequency sounds through while cutting off High Frequencies, and the High Pass Filter allows High Frequencies while cutting off Low Frequencies.

Last but not least we have the cross fader; the cross fader allows you to switch back and forth between songs or the ability to play two songs simultaneously if set in the middle. The cross fader is a great tool but can be tricky to master. Spend some time working on just getting the hang of transitioning between songs. *Quick tip: unless the songs are similar in Beats Per Minute, don't go slowly with the cross fader. Instead start turning your Low EQ knob off on the song already playing and moving the cross fader to the other song.*

CHAPTER THREE
Deciding on a mixer/controller

Finding a mixer/controller that's right for your budget

The most powerful tool(s) in any DJ's arsenal is the controller and mixer they will use. The time you put into learning your devices will be the difference between a new DJ vs a Pro. DJ equipment can be expensive, but don't let that get you down. You can do almost anything with the simple controllers out there as long as you put the time into learning it. I myself started with a simple Hercules Control Instinct; it was cheap, contained both a controller and mixer, and could handle my beginning needs. Be careful buying equipment so expensive and littered with extras that it will bog you down and prevent you from actually learning the techniques without the hardware. I honestly believe starting with a simple set up allows you to learn the basic mixing techniques every DJ needs. Don't ever let anyone's critique on your hardware get you down; everyone has their own journey on the path to being a DJ, and the equipment you can afford means nothing about your skill. Your abilities will drive you farther than any equipment.

There is no single option that works best for everyone, but there are preferences. For instance, do you want to have the ability to plug your laptop or computer in to your device, do you prefer to use a USB stick, CDs, or even hardware for vinyl. Personally, I think digital is the best option for new DJs in this day and age as we all have access to a computer; this is why I will be solely focusing on digital controllers. Be forewarned that by choosing this route you will need a DJ software to connect to your device. Most controllers meant for the computer come with a Demo or Lite versions of these software that will work, but you will most likely want to upgrade to the full version. Virtual DJ, Traktor, and Serato are among the top used software by DJs both new and old. Virtual DJ is an excellent beginning software as it is affordable, has great controller compatibility, and has a fairly simple interface allowing you to learn at a faster pace than some. While the other software have a harder learning curve, they have more features and options available to them. If you stick with the harder software you will end off with more tools available to you, but you may have a harder time getting started with it.

The cheapest option that I can recommend is the Hercules Instinct, roughly $75 and it comes with the software DJuiced. This option includes a controller and mixer all in one. You will find it lacking in functions, but for a beginning controller it will work.

Next I would suggest the Numark Mixtrack 3 for $149.99, a lot of available features makes this a great beginning controller! Although the make of the deck isn't the strongest it boasts beat pads, frequency knobs, EQ, FX pads and more!

The best medium-priced recommendation I can give is the Pioneer DDJ-SB2, $250 price tag but it comes with everything you need. Rubber pads, low latency jog wheels, trim knobs, and more. For the price this is one of the most comprehensive devices you can start with.

Now we are making a bit of a jump: if you have the money to spend, I'd recommend the Denon DJ MC7000. $1,000 price tag but this controller can do it all. It's the best controller I've seen with Serato, with so many features, 4 decks, and the ability to use multiple USBs to switch between sets. I know you are probably thinking you will never be able to afford hardware with prices like that, but you will. Save a little bit of money from each gig you get paid for and eventually you will get there.

On top of all of these choices, you will have to get a laptop. I'm going to let you decide whether or not you want a PC or a Mac. Both operating systems have their ups and downs. I personally use a PC for DJing and you can get some new models for about $100. Does yours have to be the best, most expensive laptop available, no. It just has to be able to run with no problems. I personally close all applications in the background before setting up my equipment to allow all CPU usage to go to my DJ software.

CHAPTER FOUR
Controller Techniques

<u>Quick methods to get you up and running</u>

I say this at the beginning in case you, the reader, is following step by step. Always record every time you mix or practice or even play around with your controller. This allows you to listen right afterwards and find mistakes that you might not have picked up on while mixing. Maybe your cue point is a little off, or your fade time was too fast; whatever it is, recording it and listening to your work allows you to improve and become a pro. Okay now that I got that out of the way, let's proceed.

Make sure you have the controller and software linked together; this includes being able to control your DJ software from your controller. If the software is not responding to your actions you may need to go into software settings and find the section for external inputs (controllers, mixers, etc.). Once you have that all working, find two songs in your music library with a similar BPM and spend time getting familiar with the songs, set your cues before and after drops, during the chorus or any other part of a song you want to swing back to. Next, I want you to get comfortable cross fading between the two songs. You should be able to confidently transition between the two songs with ease; slowly start adding in cue points and cross fading between the two to start making a mix. After you feel confident in your abilities, go through your library and start adding cue points to songs you wish to add to a mix. After this you can start adding in loops, samples and more, but don't overdo it on the effects!

13

Not every song has to be mixed after the first drop; sometimes the best moments allow a song to play out while you cue up the next song. A longer mix with better transitions always beats a short mix with choppy mixes. Make sure you can keep a rhythm with your mix so that it progresses as it goes on, end on a high note on some mixes to later show promoters you can open for bigger acts and hype the crowd for them. While everyone wants to get the dance floor poppin', you have to show that you will be able to play for your time slot. Even your favorite artists have started out opening for someone else bigger than them at first.

CHAPTER FIVE
Creating your first real mix

<u>The First Mix You make Matters!</u>

Now when I say this, I don't mean your other mixes don't matter or that they were pointless because they are necessary to get you up to this point. If you put out garbage mixes no one is going to want to hire you, so when it comes time for your first mix to post, I want you to have all of the techniques from the previous chapter mastered as well as your knowledge and layout of the set for this mix; there should be no background distractions (animals, TV, significant others, etc.). The most important thing is that you need to have fun; the listener can feel when you are enjoying what you are doing versus an overly rehearsed set of songs. When you have fun your audience has fun, and this will translate well later on when you've got promoters looking to book you.

This mix should encompass the genres you are looking to focus on and play specifically, because there is nothing worse than showing up to a gig and being told to play a music type you weren't prepared for. You will be miserable, your audience will be miserable, and most importantly you might lose your contact with that venue or club. Don't be afraid of feedback from anyone you meet, take all negatives as constructive criticism and further your skills as a DJ. You're never going to please everyone so don't change for anyone, but take to mind advice and test its compatibility with yourself.

When you finish making the mix, sit down in a quiet place, put on headphones and listen to the mix you just finished. Was there a misstep somewhere, did you accidentally come in too early fading in one song over the other? If so, I highly recommend you go back to your DJ workstation and bust out the mix again, but this time correcting your mistakes. I know how frustrating it can be to finish a set and then hear all of the problems afterwards on a mix you thought went perfectly, but that's what makes a pro versus a hobbyist. The pro only puts out the best work they can create and continues to better their work. It's the reason why some musicians take years on an album; you have to get the sound right before you can put it out for everyone else.

CHAPTER SIX
Finding Your Streaming Site

What site do I begin with?!?

It can be daunting trying to find what site to upload to and where to put your mixes with so many available options. Now with all of the benefits of having multiple streaming sites comes negatives; if you open up an account on every site but fail to keep posting on a regular basis to all platforms then you will lose followers. I know it sounds rough but people are habitual, we all like to follow patterns, no matter who we are we all do it. When you stop posting on a site that some fans use exclusively, then you are alienating that crowd as they won't seek you out on other platforms. They will just seek out other artists on their current platform. So before you open lots of accounts, look for ones you will actually be interested and active in on a regular basis.

• **SoundCloud**: Best site for Uploading mixes for EDM, Trap, Rap, Drum n' Bass, Dubstep and more. Completely free to sign up and upload your mixes, there is a paid option for pro but the free allows you to do everything you need. This site allows for users to follow you and get updates in a social media type format for all of your new music.

• **Mixcloud**: Mixcloud is a great alternative to SoundCloud and has a huge base of starting out DJs, it's completely free and can be embedded in websites or used by radio stations. It doesn't have as many users, but you can still expect lots of listeners through here.

• **Beatport**: Beatport allows you to sell your mixes; yes that's right sell them. If you are continuously working and

17

putting out new quality mixes with this website, you will have an opportunity to make a little money on the side.

- **Bandcamp**: This streaming site is best for rap, trap, and underground beats but has a huge userbase of listeners to all sorts of genres. All artist profiles are free on this website as well.
- **Audiomack**: Another big site for up and coming artists, this one is very similar to SoundCloud in its music genres and listeners. Like the others, artist profiles are free and allow for unlimited uploads to your profile.
- **Louder.me**: A fairly new site in the music industry, this site allows you to upload your music and have it compete against other people's songs. It's great promotion that allows their userbase to hear your music and is completely free to use.
- **YouTube**: I know you're probably reading this and going "what, YouTube? No way!" but yes way, many artists have gotten their start on YouTube. It's free, boasts the biggest userbase out of this entire list and allows users to subscribe to you so they can see every new song you post. Besides, YouTube allows you to post music videos and really impress club venues with your views.
- **DailyMotion**: Similar to YouTube in that it is a free upload site for videos to accommodate your music. This site has a huge userbase of music uploaders so it's a great market to tap into if you are already making videos for YouTube anyways.

CHAPTER SEVEN
Your Stage Name

<u>The name, is it that important?</u>

Why yes, yes it is. Your stage name will encompass everything you do marketing-wise from here on out. Your profile or channel from the streaming sites of last chapter should have your stage name in it and if it's already taken add "TheReal" to it to make it official. An example would be @TheRealDDGraston versus @DDGraston. This implies that your profile is more important and not a fake one. So, do you have to change your name to make it big? No, in fact if your name flows nicely you should use it. Look at Martin Garrix or Dillon Francis, they use their own name and have made it big, but their name flows nicely. It's not awkward to say, and studies show that people with the X and S sound in their name are perceived as cooler.

Now if your name, like mine, doesn't sound as good as some people's, then you could look at doing a name similar to DJ Khaled or DJ Carnage, simply one name with "DJ" in front of it. Nothing hard about that, I could be DJ D, but the problem is many people have done that now and there are most likely loads of DJ Ds. If you spend all of your time marketing a brand name that someone else is using, you may find all of your efforts have been wasted as they are profiting from your marketing. Before you decide officially on any name do yourself a favor and search around the Internet if that name is in use, even if you change it later on down the line it could come back to haunt you later if people confuse you with another musician.

One of the best ways you can distinguish yourself is by using a made up or obscure word as your name as no one else will likely have it taken. Look at Galantis, Skrillex, or Flux Pavilion. They didn't have to worry about anyone having the same name (except for copycats later on) because the name was unique. It makes advertising easier, it makes remembering who you are easier, and it distinguishes yourself from every other artist out there. Be warned if you do go this route, make your name something easy to spell. When someone goes to look you up on the Internet but can't find you because they are spelling it wrong, you lose out on listens, views, and potential future fans.

The last option, name-wise, is to do a play on words. Plays on words are big in the DJ community. From famous DJs such as RL Grime, Alison Wonderland, or even Zomboy. All of these names take a really well-known name and add a twist to make it their own. Plays on words are popular as people can better recall a name similar to one they already know of. Alison Wonderland will always be easy to remember because many people know of the book and movie titled Alice in Wonderland.

So, spend time working out the right name for your music; if you are working with tropical house a happy-sounding name will ensure listeners know what they are listening to. No one is going to want to listen to a pop DJ named Psycho Murder Killers, so choose something that fits your music personality. Most importantly, choose something you like. Don't just choose a name that you think people will like, it is about to become your brand and you are about to become that name. You have to feel comfortable with the name that's going to define your music career!

CHAPTER EIGHT
Finding your First Gig

How do I get booked?

There's no simple be all end all answer that makes every club or bar want you, but that doesn't mean you can't make it there with these simple techniques to getting booked. When you're starting out getting the first gigs, it's going to be hard. You're going to have to be out there pounding on the pavement, knocking on every door of all the clubs, bars, and nightlife venues in your immediate and not so immediate area. You're going to want to show up prepared, showing up with a pre-printed concert flyer with your name and a placeholder for the venue's name will make them see that you are serious and are willing to market yourself for them in order to fill the venue. It can be as simple as a cloudy background with your stage name as a headliner and placeholders for other talents or a pre-designed flyer that you will use for a tour of shows.

On top of having the flyer, you've got to have a card with your name and link to your streaming sites as well as a CD with your best (and most listened to) mixes. Having all of this available allows the promoter to do some background searching into your music and style, as well as your listening numbers. Just because you have low listening numbers to your mixes will not disqualify you, having great mixes that you took the time to perfect will always come out on top. This is why I was so adamant about making sure your mixes are great before uploading, as this is what you will be judged on whether you get the part or not. A great tactic for getting the job is to go in on the venue's slow nights and ask to speak to the owner or manager. Tell them your ideas on how you can turn that slow night around next week when you are playing at their venue. Be proactive with the promoter, tell him you will fill up the place and get people in to the club night after night. No is not an answer you will take, be persistent but not annoying.

When you finally have your first gig booked you need to invite everyone you know; you can't be shy or embarrassed, you need to be proud of all of the hard work you have put in this far to get here. You've made it farther than most hobbyists ever get by actually being booked. The sky is the limit here because you've got your first gig! Don't be afraid to take a super low paying or not paying gig at all, you just need this one as experience, allowing you to move on and get paid better as you progress.

Setting up your own website also helps in getting your first gig; there are lots of free and cheap options out there to help you keep costs down to a minimum. By having this site, it shows the person in charge of booking talent that you mean business and have an upcoming internet presence. This website should link to all of your media sites, your contact info and more for the promoters to get to you.

CHAPTER NINE
Marketing and Branding

<u>Branding is (Mostly) Everything</u>

Skill will always beat out everything, but branding is a close second with DJing. If no one can find you, then they won't be able to listen to you and you will never get booked. Your stage name (see chapter 7) is your new brand, it's your baby, and like a loving parent you want to see your brand grow. So how do you grow it? You advertise, you market, you sell merchandise on your personal website, you do giveaways to your followers on social media. You've got to do everything you can to get yourself out there ahead of everyone else. Am I saying to go out on Venice Beach and try to get everyone to listen to your mix tape because it's fire? No, maybe that's worked for some people, but I've never seen it happen in my time.

One of the best things you can do to differentiate yourself is get a logo; it doesn't have to be expensive or a daunting task. You can use the website Fiverr or TaskRabbit for around $5-$25 and have a custom logo made to suit your style and stage name. This logo should be placed on every bit of merchandise you give away, sell, whatever! The more people that remember your logo and name, the more your name will spread by word of mouth.

If you've been following along with the book so far and you are booking gigs, you should be giving out T-shirts with your name, stickers, anything you can to market yourself. You will love it for the exposure and the venue owner will love it because people love free stuff. Every time you post a giveaway on social media you will gain lots of followers but immediately lose some when the contest ends; let those ones go as the ones who stay following you are the true fans and will continue following your music.

Now hold on just a minute before you go out and spend all your money at the beginning. The MOST important thing needed from here is the logo and that could be had for cheap. The rest should all be purchased after you have solid equipment and are getting paid to DJ; you don't want to spend all of your money on merchandise and be in debt. Start off with stickers, there are many cheap deals online for bulk and they can be passed out anywhere. A little goes a long way in terms of merchandise if you go about it correctly.

Another great way to market your brand and your music is to set up a website; on your website you should have a link to all of your social media so fans can follow you across all mediums, a download section with free wallpapers of your logo that you previously had made, an input box for listeners to sign up for updates (send a mass email to this list of emails anytime you upload a new mix for guaranteed listeners), and a contact section so promoters for bars, clubs and festivals can contact you to book more gigs.

CHAPTER TEN
Outro

The Last Set

No matter what you do you are going to get people who doubt you, people who don't like your music, and people who want to see you fail. But you can't let them get you down. It may take you longer than 60 days but by following the steps outlined in this book you will get there. First you need to get your equipment; without it you will never be able to mix anything. Find hardware and software that you like as this will affect everything you can or cannot do. Spend 2 weeks working on mixing and getting used to your controller and software. In those weeks you should be repeating all basic techniques until you have them down to a T.

Next you want to record your first pre-planned set; it should have cue points already set and you should complete it distraction-free. After completing the mix, listen to it, really listen to it and be hard on yourself. Go back and fix all mistakes you made before uploading it to your chosen streaming media sites. Post your music on any social media you may have, and don't be afraid to ask friends and family to give it a listen and let you know what they think and to bump up your early listen and view counts. Once you have a few mixes posted under your stage name under all streaming sites, go to a bar or club and speak to the owner, manager, whoever is in charge. Show them all the materials you made before the event, including test flyers with your name and the venues, show them your listen counts as well as give them a card with your name, contact information, and link to all of your media sites (don't forget to tell them if you have stickers or promotional material to give out, this is a huge plus).

Once you've had your first couple of shows, draft a resume to include with all of your materials previously used showcasing your experience doing those first couple events. Feel free to include any photos you might have taken showing the crowd on any night you performed or anything else. The hardest part of our industry is getting that first gig; once you have that it becomes so much easier to continue booking and look into setting up a tour. Follow all of the steps outlined in this book and you will succeed as a DJ.

Quick answer to a question I get asked a lot, should you get a talent manager by the time the 60 days are up? I'm not knocking any agents, but when you are just starting out if you are willing to put in the work getting out there and setting up gigs then an agent will be a waste of money. If however you are shy, nervous, or just don't have the time to actually call or make appearances to land the gigs, then an agent will work great for you. They take the job of selling you if you can't sell yourself. If you can, save money and represent yourself for now. If you don't feel like it, then get yourself a reputable agent! Read all reviews and search the Internet before deciding on any specific agent as you will most likely be stuck with them for a while.

Thank you for taking the time and reading this book. I hope it has helped and continues to help your journey on to becoming a famous DJ. Please leave a review if it has helped at all to allow others to find this publication. If you would like to stay up to date on my next book, "*How To Produce Music in 60 days*" or any other future publications sign up for my newsletter at:http://eepurl.com/dxEYGz

CHAPTER ELEVEN
The Secret Chapter

The Cheat Sheet
- 2 weeks learning and mastering basic techniques
- 1 week creating your first mix playlist as well as setting cue points
- 1 week perfecting your first mix, deciding on a stage name, and choosing your streaming sites
- 2 weeks creating more mixes and perfecting them
- 2 weeks going to every venue, club and bar around and marketing yourself to them! Don't leave any place unturned, and come back if the person you need to speak to is away

*During these weeks you are not expected to spend all of your time learning, but you should look at devoting 2-3 hours a day during these 8 weeks. If you can stick to this schedule and routine you will have roughly 180 hours of expertise under your belt at the end of 60 days. You will be on your way to being a pro!

About the Author

D.D. Graston; Is a portugese american DJ, Producer and Author. He studied at the University of Nevada, Reno. He has been DJ'ing for over 7 years now, but has been an audiophile all of his life. He focuses on playing EDM, Rap, and Trap in his professional sets but has been known to play whatever music is requested. When he is not DJ'ing or writing, he enjoys activities such as spending time with his girlfriend, listening to audiobooks, and watching game of thrones with his two cats. This is D.D.'s first book to date, with his second book *How To Produce Music in 60 days* on its way.

Printed in Great
Britain
by Amazon